Samson
the strong man

Story by Penny Frank

Illustrated by Tony Morris

THE LION
STORY BIBLE

14

TRING · BELLEVILLE · SYDNEY

The Bible tells us how God chose the Israelites to be his special people. He made them a promise that he would love and care for them. But they must obey him.

This is the story of a time when the Israelites did not obey God.

God sent Samson to lead them against their enemies. You can find the story in your own Bible, in Judges chapters 13 to 16.

Copyright © 1985 Lion Publishing

Published by
Lion Publishing plc
Icknield Way, Tring, Herts, England
ISBN 0 85648 739 2
Lion Publishing Corporation
10885 Textile Road, Belleville,
Michigan 48111, USA
ISBN 0 85648 739 2
Albatross Books
PO Box 320, Sutherland, NSW 2232, Australia
ISBN 0 86760 523 5

First edition 1985

All rights reserved

Printed and bound in Hong Kong
by Mandarin Offset International (HK) Ltd

**British Library Cataloguing in
Publication Data**

Frank, Penny
 Samson, the strong man. – (The Lion
Story Bible; 14)
 1. Samson – Juvenile literature
 2. Bible stories, English – O.T. Judges
 I. Title   II. Series
 222'.320924   BS580.S15

 ISBN 0-85648-739-2

**Library of Congress Cataloging in
Publication Data**

Frank, Penny.
Samson, the strong man.
(The Lion Story Bible; 14)
 1. Samson (Judge of Israel)—Juvenile
literature. 2. Bible. O.T.—Juvenile
literature. [1. Samson (Judge of Israel)
2. Bible stories—O.T.] I. Morris, Tony,
ill. II. Title. III. Series: Frank, Penny.
Lion Story Bible; 14.
BS580.S15F69 1985   222'.320924 [B]
84-26082
ISBN 0-85648-739-2

The Israelites needed a new leader.
They had forgotten to obey God, and
they had lost all their battles.
Now the Philistines ruled over them
in the land God had given them.

The Philistines were God's enemies.
They worshipped gods made of wood
and stone, called idols.

One day God sent an angel to visit the wife of Manoah, one of the Israelites.

'You are going to have a very special baby,' the angel told her. 'When he grows up he will be a leader for God's people. God will use him to fight the Philistines.'

Manoah and his wife were very excited.

'What must we do to look after him?' they asked.

The angel told them they must let the child's hair grow long as a sign that he belonged especially to God. When he grew up, they must not allow him to drink any wine.

By the time Samson was a man he was big and very strong. Because he had obeyed God, he became the leader of the Israelites.

'It's time we turned these Philistines out of the land,' he told the Israelites. 'They are God's enemies.'

Samson went into the fields belonging to the Philistines. He tied burning sticks to the tails of some foxes. The foxes ran through the fields, and all the wheat was burned.

The Philistines were furious.

'Just wait until we catch Samson,' they said.

One day, the Philistines heard that Samson was visiting a house in the city of Gaza. They thought they could catch him at last.

They locked the gates of the city and waited silently by the city wall.

But when Samson came down the street
and saw the locked gates he did not
look worried at all.

He picked up the enormous gates with
their locks and chains, and carried them
away up the hill, outside the city walls.

The Philistines were worried.

They knew it was not going to be easy to catch Samson. He had the strength of thirty men!

They sent a beautiful woman called Delilah to pretend to be his friend.

'You must find out what makes Samson so strong,' they told her.

Samson fell in love with beautiful Delilah. He did not know she wanted to trick him into telling her his secret.

Delilah said to Samson, 'You are so strong. How could anyone tie you up so that you could not escape?'

Samson said, 'If I was tied up with the strings from seven new bows, then I would be a prisoner.'

So the Philistines gave Delilah the strings from seven new bows. She tied up Samson in his sleep. But when he woke, Samson easily broke the strings.

Delilah still did not know his secret.

'It's not fair to tell me a lie!' said
Delilah. 'Now please tell me if there
is a way you could really be tied up?'

Samson said, 'If they used new ropes
to tie me, I couldn't break those.'

So the Philistines gave Delilah some new ropes. She tied up Samson in his sleep. But, when he woke, Samson easily broke the ropes.

Delilah still did not know his secret.

'It's unkind to tease me like this!'
said Delilah. 'Now please do tell me
if there is a way you could really be
tied up.'

Samson said, 'If you use my long hair
instead of wool on your loom, then I
couldn't get away.

So, while Samson was asleep, Delilah wove his hair into the cloth on her loom. But, when he woke, he easily freed himself from the loom.

Delilah still did not know his secret.

'You are making a fool of me,' said Delilah. 'I am only asking you one simple question, and you won't tell me the truth.'

By now Samson was so tired of being asked that he told Delilah the secret.

'I am strong because I belong especially to God. Because of that, my hair has never been cut.'

Delilah waited until Samson was asleep, and cut his hair short. Then she called the Philistines.

When Samson woke up, all his strength had gone. He could not escape.

The Philistines put Samson in prison.
They chained him up. They made him
blind. And they put him to work, to
grind grain.

Samson was miserable. How he wished
he had used his special strength
properly. He knew God had wanted him
to fight the Philistines. Now there
was nothing he could do.

But then Samson felt his hair.
It was beginning to grow long again!

One day, the five Philistine kings held a great feast, with many important leaders. They called a servant to bring Samson from the prison, so that they could make fun of him.

They did not notice how long Samson's hair was now.

Samson asked the servant to lead him to the two middle pillars in the building.

'I will die with all these Philistines,' he said. 'God has given me one last chance to use my strength for him.'

He pushed the pillars so hard that the whole building fell down. At last, God's enemies were defeated.

The Lion Story Bible is made up of 52 individual stories for young readers, building up an understanding of the Bible as one story — God's story — a story for all time and all people.

The Old Testament section (numbers 1–30) tells the story of a great nation — God's chosen people, the Israelites — and God's love and care for them through good times and bad. The stories are about people who knew and trusted God. From this nation came one special person, Jesus Christ, sent by God to save all people everywhere.

Samson, the strong man comes from the Old Testament book of Judges, chapters 13 to 16. The Israelites had settled in the promised land of Canaan, but they had not kept their promise to serve and obey God. They had begun to worship the gods of the peoples around them. And those nations had invaded their land. But each time they turned to God and asked for his help he sent a leader to deliver them from their enemies. Samson was one of these great champions of Israel, sent to free them from the Philistines. Sadly, he let God down, but God gave him a second chance.

The next story in the series, number 15: *Ruth's new family*, set in these same violent times, shows God's love and care for each individual who trusts him.